MASTERS OF
HORROR

Also by Daniel Cohen

Horror in the Movies

MASTERS OF
horror

DANIEL COHEN

Illustrated with photographs

CLARION BOOKS

TICKNOR & FIELDS: A HOUGHTON MIFFLIN COMPANY

NEW YORK

PHOTO CREDITS: pages 9, 12, 19, 43, 44, and 82, courtesy of Universal Pictures; page 89, from the MGM release *Dr. Jekyll and Mr. Hyde* © 1932 Paramount Publix Corporation, copyright renewed 1959 by Loew's Inc.; page 103, © Unangst, courtesy of Kirby McCauley Ltd.

Clarion Books
Ticknor & Fields, a Houghton Mifflin Company
Copyright © 1984 by Daniel Cohen

Printed in the U.S.A.

Library of Congress Cataloging in Publication Data
Cohen, Daniel.
Masters of horror.

Includes index.
Summary: Profiles four superstars of horror films, and discusses notable contributions by directors, writers, special effects and make-up artists, and other actors.
1. Horror films — Juvenile literature. [1. Motion pictures — Biography. 2. Horror films] I. Title.
PN1995.9H6C63   1984   791.43'09'0916 [920]   83-14402
ISBN 0-89919-221-1

Q 10 9 8 7 6 5 4 3 2 1

TO BORIS

CONTENTS

WELCOME TO TRANSYLVANIA

Welcome back, horror fans.

Or if you are new to horror fandom, just plain welcome.

We horror film fans like to talk about the films and remember our favorites. We enjoy swapping trivia. Question: Who played the Frankenstein monster in *Frankenstein Meets the Wolf Man*? Answer: Bela Lugosi.

Horror films have been around since films began. They have always been popular. But a lot of people won't admit they enjoy such films. And if you say you are a fan, you get funny looks from some people. You're not supposed to enjoy films like *that*. They are supposed to be bad for you.

Just like Rodney Dangerfield says, horror films "don't get no respect."

Do you know what film won the Academy Award for best picture in 1931? It was an epic of the Old West called *Cimarron*. The stars were Richard Dix, Irene Dunne and Edna May Oliver. Did you ever see *Cimarron*? Do you

1

know anyone who has ever seen it? Did you ever hear of it before? I'll bet you answered no to all of those questions.

There was another film that came out that year that you have seen. It's a film that almost everyone has seen — *Frankenstein*. And I'll bet you will have no trouble remembering who starred in that.

How about *Cavalcade*? That took best picture in 1933. Remember it? Of course not. But you do remember another picture that came out in 1933 — *King Kong*.

This is a book for horror film fans and for those of you who would like to be fans. Or for those of you who happen to know a fan and want to be able to talk to him or her. The book will help you relive some of the great moments of terror. And it may tip you off to some horrific delights you have not yet enjoyed.

You will learn more about the people who brought you all of those wonderful frights. And you can pick up some bits and pieces of information with which to stump your fellow fans. Question: What actor appeared in the original *Dracula, Frankenstein* and *The Mummy*? Answer: Edward Van Sloan.

From time to time in the book, I talk about "cult movies." Or about actors and actresses who have become "cult figures." That has nothing to do with joining a religious group and selling flowers on the street. A cult film is one that has a really fanatical following. Cultists will stay up to any hour of the night to see one of their favorites on the *Late, Late Show*. They'll watch it even if they have seen the picture ten or twenty times before.

Practically every horror film ever made has some cult following. But some, such as *King Kong* or *Halloween*, have bigger cults than others. The king of the cult films is *The Rocky Horror Picture Show*. Sometimes a film will develop a cult following not because people think it is so good, but because they think it is so bad. *The Attack of the Killer Tomatoes* is a good example.

The same is true with a cult figure. Cultists will go to see their favorite in anything, no matter how bad the film or how small the part.

I love horror films. I hate to hear people put them down. But I don't love all horror films equally. I think some are better than others. I think some actors and actresses are better than others. I have strong opinions. One of them is that I don't think the value of a horror film can be measured solely in the amount of blood that is spilled. Nor can it be judged by the number of eyes that are gouged, right before *your* eyes. I think that sometimes what you *don't* see can be more frightening than what you do see.

I don't try to hide my opinions. As a result you will probably disagree with a lot that I have to say. If you are a real fan, you may find yourself yelling at this book from time to time. That's fine. If sports fans can yell, so can we.

Strong feelings — that's what fandom is all about.

Boris Karloff

1

KARLOFF –
KING OF HORROR

Who is the number one star of horror films — ever? For me, there can be only one possible answer to that question — Boris Karloff.

I know there are other candidates, such as Christopher Lee or Vincent Price. But Karloff has the edge on all the others.

He was the king of horror films during the 1930s, the Golden Age of horror films. And he created two of the most memorable monsters in film history — the Frankenstein monster and the Mummy.

He was also a first-rate actor. He could and did play many nonhorror parts. But he specialized in horror films and appeared in over fifty of them.

Boris Karloff almost always gave a good performance. Like all actors, Karloff needed to work. He had to take the parts that were offered him. So he appeared in a lot of B movies, and in some really embarrassing trash. But he always did his job. Often his performance was the best thing about a film. He was an actor who cared about his work. He cared about his audience. He never let us down.

So with all due respect to Lee, Price, and the rest, for me Boris Karloff will always be number one.

Karloff seemed to have burst on the movie scene in 1931. That's the year he played the monster in the original *Frankenstein*. But he was not exactly an overnight success. At the time he had been picked to play the monster, he was forty-four years old. He had been acting on the stage and as a bit player in films for over twenty years. Yet, after all that time, he was still practically unknown. Now and then, Karloff had to take a job as a laborer or truck driver to support himself.

Boris Karloff was born on November 23, 1887, in a suburb of London, England. The name he was born with was William Henry Pratt. He was the youngest of eight children. Most of the members of his family became diplomats. But he wasn't interested. He didn't do very well at school either.

In 1909, young William Henry Pratt sailed for Canada. He tried farming, and failed at that. So he decided to become an actor. He went to far-western Canada and landed a job with a touring stock company. Western Canada was the frontier. The audiences were not very demanding. He didn't know much about acting. However, he was very good at learning lines quickly. That was a vital asset in the sort of acting he did. In one year, he played over one hundred different parts.

In 1918 Karloff found himself in Los Angeles. But it

was harder than ever for him to find work on the stage. Many theaters were closing because of competition from the movies. Like many other actors, Karloff decided to try to work in films. He started by appearing in crowd scenes. He was paid five dollars a day. Over the years he worked his way up to minor parts. He had a kind of sinister look, so he usually got parts as a villain. He played gangsters, murderous sailors, mysterious Indians. No matter how small the part, Karloff always seemed to give it a little extra.

Karloff started in silent films. By the late 1920s, sound had come to films. During his years on the stage, Karloff had developed his voice, and he could sound very cultured or very frightening. In the sound era, his voice became a major asset to his film career.

By 1930, Boris Karloff was working steadily. He was making about a picture a month. And he was appearing in an occasional play. He was pretty well-known in the film community. But he was no star, and he didn't think that he would ever become one.

In mid-1931 Karloff was working at Universal Studios. Universal was to become the home of horror in the 1930s. One day, while he was eating in the studio lunchroom, he was told that the director James Whale was eating at a nearby table and wanted to talk to him.

As a director, Whale was considered a hot property at that moment. Universal had brought him over from England. Whale was assigned to direct a film made from Mary Shelley's novel *Frankenstein*. The director was fascinated by Karloff's face. He found it brutal, yet sensitive. He asked Karloff to try out for the part of the monster.

Neither Karloff nor Whale was originally supposed to have anything to do with *Frankenstein*. Universal Studios had assigned the French director Robert Florey to the picture. The part of the monster was to be played by Bela Lugosi. Lugosi had just been a huge success in *Dracula*.

Lugosi didn't like the part. He didn't want to work under all that heavy makeup. The studio was also having second thoughts about Florey. So Florey and Lugosi went on to make another film. Whale and Karloff did *Frankenstein*. And the film made both of them famous.

When you see *Frankenstein*, you get the impression that the monster is huge and massive. But Boris Karloff was a very average-sized man. In fact, he was rather thin. The impression of size is created by makeup and photography.

Karloff wore built-up boots and a heavily padded coat. His jacket and pants were cut short. This gave the illusion that he was so big, he was bursting out of his clothes. Whale was careful not to have Karloff photographed standing right next to anyone taller than he was. The actor who played Dr. Frankenstein was taller than Karloff. It would never do to have the monster-maker taller than the monster. When you next see *Frankenstein*, notice how the camera was used to make Karloff look taller.

Makeup for the monster was created by Universal's top

Karloff as the Frankenstein monster

makeup artist, Jack Pierce. Karloff was given a flat-topped skull, scars, stitches, and electrodes in his neck. He did not wear a mask. You can see the actor's face beneath the makeup. His face could reflect rage and pain. Karloff was able to make the creature both frightening and sympathetic.

Physically, the part of the monster was very demanding. Shooting began at 5:30 in the morning. Makeup took three hours, and the costume was very uncomfortable. The film was shot in midsummer, and wearing the heavily padded monster costume left Karloff exhausted and soaking with sweat, after just a few hours. Sometimes Karloff didn't know how he was going to make it through the day. But he always did. And it was worth it. The film was a huge hit. The studio originally thought that the romantic leads, Colin Clive and Mae Clark, would be the stars. The public felt differently. They made the star Boris Karloff.

Karloff was grateful. He said that after twenty years of acting, now he finally knew where his next meal was coming from.

Boris Karloff is always thought of as the Frankenstein monster. Actually he played the role only three times. The second Frankenstein film *The Bride of Frankenstein* (made in 1935) was, if anything, even better than the original. And Karloff, as the monster, got to say a few words.

His third turn as the monster was in *Son of Frankenstein*, made in 1938. Though *Son* wasn't quite up to the other two Frankenstein films, it wasn't bad at all. In this film, the monster played a somewhat minor role. It was rumored that Karloff had been injured and that the heavy costume was causing him so much pain that he had to limit his role. Whatever the reason, Karloff was over fifty at the time. The part of the monster took too much out of him. He swore he would never play it again. And he didn't. (Years later, he made one brief appearance as the monster on a TV show. But that hardly counts).

Many others have played the role of the Frankenstein monster. But the part always has, and always will, belong to Boris Karloff.

The second great Karloff role was as the Mummy in the 1932 film called, of course, *The Mummy*. Actually Karloff appears as the Mummy — the undead thing, wrapped in rotting bandages — only briefly, at the beginning of the film. But the makeup, again designed by Jack Pierce, is very effective. Pierce was careful not to wrap Karloff's face.

Unwrapped, the Mummy takes the disguise of Ardet Bey, an Egyptian archaeologist. As Ardet Bey, Karloff is stiff and sinister, more of an evil magician than a monster.

The Mummy provides a good example of why Boris Karloff is superior to so many other horror film actors. Karloff played the Mummy only once, but there have been many other mummy films. In these later films, Karloff's followers and imitators act as if they were nothing more than wrapped robots. They would strangle their victims. Karloff didn't have to strangle anyone. He didn't even have to touch his victims. He was supposed to pro-

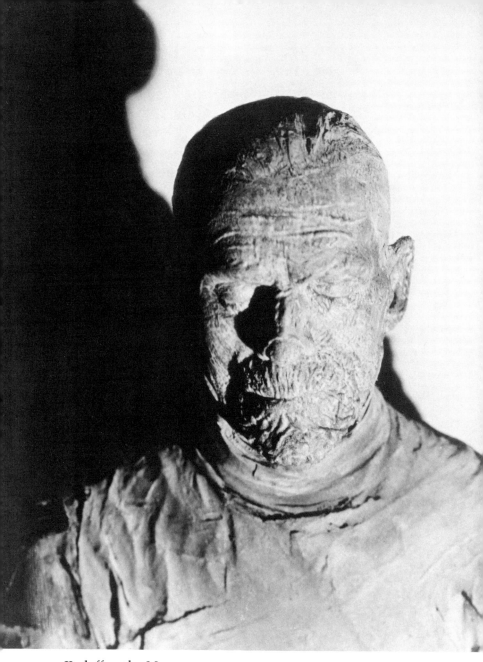

Karloff as the Mummy

ject an evil force that allowed him to control and even kill people at a distance. Karloff played the part so well, that he made the audience believe in his power. He didn't need trick photography, he didn't even need heavy makeup. He did it with his voice, his deep penetrating gaze, and with a few simple movements of his head and arms.

Immediately after his great success with *Frankenstein*, Karloff made two other major horror films in addition to *The Mummy*. The first was *The Old Dark House* (1932). He plays a mute, sometimes murderous butler. Once again Karloff's thin frame was heavily padded to make him look bigger.

The second major film was *The Mask of Fu Manchu* (1933). In this film he played Dr. Fu Manchu, an evil Chinese genius out to rule the world. For a while Karloff seemed to specialize in Chinese roles. He played the bandit Wu Yen Fang in *West of Shanghai* (1937), and the Chinese detective Mr. Wong, in a series of films. Even with makeup, Karloff did not look the least bit Chinese. But there was war in China when these films were made. That part of the world was in the news a great deal. The Hollywood studios figured that films with Chinese subjects would be popular.

While Boris Karloff will forever be thought of as the monster, the role he played most frequently was that of the "mad scientist." He was always Professor or Doctor somebody. He was Professor Morlant in *The Ghoul* (1933) and Dr. Janos Rukh in *The Invisible Ray* (1936). He played Dr. Lawrence in *The Man Who Lived Again*

(1936), Dr. Sartorius in *Juggernaut* (1936), and Dr. Savaard in *The Man They Could Not Hang* (1939). He was Dr. Sovac in *Black Friday* (1940), Dr. Kravaal in *The Man With Nine Lives* (1940), and Dr. John Garth in *Before I Hang* (1940). He appeared as Dr. Adrian in *The Ape* (1940), Dr. Julian Blair in *The Devil Commands* (1940) and Dr. Bolton in *Corridors of Blood* (1963). He was Prof. John Mayer in *The Incredible Invasion*, one of the last films he made. It was released after his death.

In *Frankenstein 1970*, Karloff took the part of Baron Victor von Frankenstein, a modern descendant of the old monster maker. That is the closest he ever came to playing that most celebrated of all mad scientists, Dr. Frankenstein.

In *House of Frankenstein* (1944) Karloff plays neither Dr. Frankenstein nor the monster. He is still a mad scientist, Dr. Gustav Niemann. This film often turns up on TV. If you haven't seen it yet, you probably will sooner or later. It is a good example of how Karloff was often much better than his material. *House of Frankenstein* is a pretty silly film. Today's audience is more likely to laugh than scream. Most of the cast seem to be just going through the motions. But Karloff delivers a first-rate, creepy performance.

Karloff is best known for his films, but he had started as a stage actor. He returned to the stage in 1940 in the comic-horror play *Arsenic and Old Lace*. He played a murderous madman called Jonathan. Jonathan killed people who told him he looked like Boris Karloff. The play was a huge success and ran for three years. Unfortunately he was not able to do the film version of the play.

Karloff also often did radio shows, and later he appeared on television. As a result of his radio shows, Karloff's voice became almost as familiar as his face. Every impressionist of the forties and fifties did a Boris Karloff imitation.

Sometimes he played a comic parody of the sinister Boris Karloff. Or he was the butt of comedians' jokes. "How much do you charge to haunt a house?" Groucho Marx asked him. On radio and TV, he appeared mostly in mystery or horror shows. But he also did a lot of straight nonhorror drama as well. He even showed up on quiz shows. The quiz programs showed the public what Karloff's fellow actors had known for years: Boris Karloff was a highly intelligent and very knowledgeable man.

Karloff hosted his own TV series, *Thriller,* which still turns up on reruns now and then. And he did a number of successful Broadway shows. He played the comic villain Captain Hook in a 1950 adaptation of *Peter Pan.*

But Karloff always returned to the films. Sometimes he appeared in third-rate low-budget shockers. Sometimes he played in films like *The Ghost in the Invisible Bikini* (1966) that were really embarrassing. Even as an old man in poor health, he could deliver a first-rate performance. In *Targets* (1968) Karloff plays Byron Orlok, an aging horror star confronted with a mad sniper. *Targets* is considered one of the best low-budget films ever made.

Boris Karloff said that he intended to die "with his boots and greasepaint on." He believed that if he retired, he would die within a few months. He was still making films when he was over eighty. In his last few films, he was often so weak and ill that he had to play his part from a wheelchair.

Boris Karloff died in England in 1969. He had just finished filming an episode for a TV show. He had indeed died with his boots and greasepaint on.

Aside from the obvious Karloff films like the Frankenstein series and *The Mummy*, here are a few others that you might look for: *The Tower of London* (1939), *The Body Snatcher* (1945), and *Bedlam* (1946). Also look for one of his later films, *Black Sabbath* (1964). *Black Sabbath* is the only film in which the old master of horror plays a vampire!

2

BELA LUGOSI –
THE MAN WHO WAS DRACULA

In 1930 Universal Studios decided to do a screen version of the novel *Dracula*. The director had already been chosen: Tod Browning. The choice of an actor to play the vampire count from Transylvania seemed obvious. Who else but the man who was then the reigning king of horror films — Lon Chaney?

Chaney had already played a vampire, and very effectively too, in a silent film called *London After Midnight* (1927). Browning had directed that film. He and Chaney had worked well together.

Chaney had been a big star in silent films. For a while, though, he held out against appearing in sound films. But he finally made the transition with *The Unholy Three*. Unlike many silent stars, Lon Chaney had an excellent speaking voice.

Why didn't Lon Chaney ever play Dracula? During the filming of *The Unholy Three*, Chaney discovered he had cancer. He died within a few months.

Tod Browning now had a script for the film of Dracula,

Bela Lugosi

Lugosi as Dracula

but no lead. Once again there seemed an obvious choice. The novel *Dracula* had been made into a play. The play had run successfully in New York for over a year. The movie script was based heavily on the play. The star of the play was a Hungarian actor. He had been born with the name Béla Blaskó, but took the stage name Bela Lugosi.

Lugosi had been a successful actor in Hungary. When he first came to America, he appeared mainly in Hungarian-language plays. He also had a few minor film roles. *Dracula* was his first major play in English. It was a great success for him. Universal asked him to come to Hollywood and recreate his vampire role on the screen. He agreed immediately.

The film *Dracula* was an immense, and immediate, hit. One picture had suddenly made Bela Lugosi the new star of horror films.

A lot of other actors have played Dracula since then. Some people think Christopher Lee did the best job in the 1960s. My personal favorite is Louis Jourdan. He played Dracula in a British-made TV series that was shown widely in the U.S. a few years ago.

But no one ever can or ever will eclipse the memory of Bela Lugosi's Dracula. He didn't just play Dracula, he *was* Dracula. You can't picture Dracula without seeing Lugosi in cape and evening clothes.

Lugosi's Dracula doesn't look at all like the count described in the original novel. In the novel, Dracula was a tall old man with a white mustache. While he dressed all in black, there was nothing about a cape. Even the heavy accent is all Lugosi. Dracula in the book spoke excellent English.

None of that makes a bit of difference. When you think of Dracula, you think of Lugosi with the slicked down black hair and the cape. You think of him saying "Good E-e-e-evening."

As the reigning king of horror in 1931, Lugosi was offered the part of the monster in Universal's next big horror project, *Frankenstein*. He turned it down. We already know who starred in *Frankenstein* as a result.

Lugosi chose to take the part of Dr. Mirakle in *Murders in the Rue Morgue* (1932). The film was supposed to be based on a tale by Edgar Allan Poe about a mad doctor in Paris who kept a killer ape. It was obviously meant to be a big production. The sets are very elaborate and effective. But the production is also very sloppy. The ape is sometimes a man in a monkey suit. Sometimes it's a real ape, or rather, *several* very different-looking apes. A lot of the picture doesn't make any sense at all. There is a rumor that the whole thing was shot in a mere three days. The rumor probably isn't true. But it could be.

Lugosi plays Dr. Mirakle almost exactly the same way he played Dracula. The film might almost be called "Dracula Goes to Paris." But even so, his performance is very menacing. And Lugosi is by far the best thing in the film. With all its faults, *Murders in the Rue Morgue* was still a big success.

But now Hollywood of the early 1930s had two kings of horror — Bela Lugosi and Boris Karloff. Naturally, Universal Studios wanted to bring the pair together. And it did. The first film they made was *The Black Cat* (1934). Lugosi played a relatively sympathetic character. Karloff was the really evil one. In *The Raven* (1936) it was Lugosi's turn to be the bad guy. Karloff is his deformed, and sometimes unwilling, assistant. The same year both appeared in a science fiction–horror film called *The Invisible Ray*. In this picture, Karloff is given a much bigger part and more prominent billing. By 1936 he was the bigger star.

The pair appeared together in other films. Karloff was to dominate Lugosi in all future films except one — and a very surprising one. The film is *Son of Frankenstein*. Karloff once again is the monster. But Bela Lugosi steals the film. He plays Ygor, the crazed peasant who really controls the monster. Ygor had been hanged for grave robbing. But the hanging didn't kill him. It just left him with a crooked neck — and a bad outlook on life.

Lugosi wears a full beard and shaggy old clothes as Ygor. He is not the smooth Dracula type. He cringes and whines. But he is nevertheless very menacing. Lugosi's heavy middle-European accent works well in this part. Next to Dracula, Ygor is Lugosi's best character.

Throughout the 1930s, Karloff and Lugosi's careers paralleled one another. Karloff was the more careful, though. He chose a variety of roles. Some of them were in nonhorror films. More and more, Lugosi took anything that was offered to him. These were almost always horror films, and often not very good ones. He even played the Frankenstein monster, a part he had once rejected, in *Frankenstein Meets the Wolf Man* (1943). It was a very poor film.

One of Lugosi's problems may have been that he was a limited actor. He looked and acted the same in practically every part he played. Another problem was his heavy Hungarian accent. Karloff said that Lugosi had never taken the trouble to learn to speak English properly. His accent was fine when playing Dracula or Ygor.

But in *White Zombie* (1932) he played Legendre, an evil Frenchman. His attempt at a French accent was absolutely ridiculous.

During the 1940s and 1950s Lugosi's career ran steadily downhill. The films he appeared in were worse and worse. They were not just B films. They were Z films with titles like *Bela Lugosi Meets a Brooklyn Gorilla* and *Mother Riley Meets the Vampire.* He wasn't menacing on the screen anymore. People laughed at him. The vampire that had once frightened them had become a joke.

Lugosi wound up working with director Edward D. Wood, Jr. Wood is generally considered to be the worst director in history. Lugosi's final film was a Wood classic called *Plan 9 from Outer Space* (1956). Actually, Lugosi died long before the film was finished. So Wood hired his own wife's chiropractor to be Lugosi's double. The chiropractor didn't look or sound at all like Lugosi. He played the part holding a cape over his face. That will give you some idea of what kind of a picture this was. *Plan 9 from Outer Space* is so bad that it has become a cult classic. Cultists practically roll in the aisles with laughter when they see it.

Somehow I can't laugh. I find it all very sad. Lugosi may never have been a great actor. But he did create one of the great horror characters of all times. He does not deserve to be laughed at, no matter how far he had fallen.

Bela Lugosi died on August 16, 1956. He was buried in his Dracula tuxedo and cape as he had requested. Bela Lugosi was, and always will be, Count Dracula. He is immortal.

3

CHRISTOPHER LEE –
DRACULA REBORN

Yes, Dracula for me will always be Bela Lugosi. But kids growing up in the 1960s usually first met Dracula in a Christopher Lee movie. Lee's Dracula was very different from Lugosi's.

Christopher Lee was a taller, more imposing, actor. His accent was British, not Hungarian. The difference between the two Draculas, however, was much more than physical appearances. When Christopher Lee bit into a victim, his fangs dripped bright red blood. The blood slobbered over his chin and down his chest. His eyes glowed blood red. When a stake was driven through Christopher Lee's heart, the blood spurted out in a gory fountain. When he was struck by the rays of the morning sun, or confronted with a cross, you could see him rot and turn into a greenish, putrid puddle before your very eyes. In the original *Dracula*, Bela Lugosi died off-camera and out of view.

The difference between the two interpretations of Dracula tells you a lot about the changes that took place

Christopher Lee

Lee as Dracula

in the making of horror films between the 1930s and the 1950s. In the 1930s, Hollywood's Universal Studios was the home of horror. In the 1950s, horror's new home was Hammer Films in Britain. Karloff was the king of horror for Universal. Lee was to become the king of horror for Hammer and the world.

Like Karloff, Lee was no overnight success. Lee was born in England in 1922. He began playing bit parts in films right after the end of World War II. It was ten years before he got his first big break in horror films. And like Karloff, he played the Frankenstein monster in his first horror film. It was released in 1957.

The film was made by Hammer Films, a small British studio. For years Hammer had limped along making minor films. Most movie studios were in financial trouble in the 1950s. The problem was, of course, competition from television.

Hammer decided that the time was ripe to give the public a new series of horror films. They decided to re-make all the old classics like *Frankenstein* and *Dracula*. But why would people pay to see remakes of films that they could see for free on TV?

Hammer had to give the public something they could not get on TV. So they gave moviegoers a number of things. First, they shot their film in color. All the old horror classics had been made in black-and-white. And color TV was hardly known in 1957. Then there was the background. The old horror films had been shot inside Hollywood studios. Hammer went out and used real old houses and castles. Hammer horror films looked much more realistic. But most of all, Hammer gave the public graphic violence and visual shocks.

Movie special effects had improved in the twenty-five years since the original *Dracula*. What the public would accept on the movie screen had changed too. At one time, a graphically violent scene simply would have been banned in Britain. It would probably not have been shown in a lot of places in the U.S. either. But by the late 1950s, the film was not only shown, it was extremely popular.

Originally, Hammer horror films were thought too violent to be shown on TV. When they did appear, they were usually heavily edited. But that has changed as well. Today you can see uncut Hammer horrors on the home screen. Every drop of blood is left in. That gives you another idea of how attitudes toward horror films have changed.

The first of Hammer horrors was called *Curse of Frankenstein* (1957). Like the Karloff film, it was based on the novel by Mary Shelley. In fact it followed the original novel a little more closely.

Lee was chosen to play the monster. Hammer could use the Frankenstein story. That had been written way back in 1816. But the studio could not use the type of makeup that had been used on Karloff, or anything close. Universal Studios was quick to sue anyone who tried to do that. So Lee was given a makeup job that made his face look like a pulpy mass. He also didn't have a great deal to do in the film. In fact, *Curse of Frankenstein*

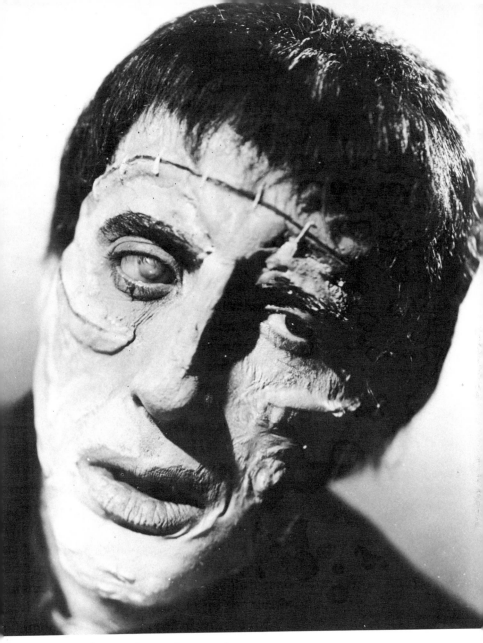

Lee as the Frankenstein monster

really wasn't a very good film. But there was no way to argue with its box office success.

Dracula, released the following year, was much better. In *Dracula*, the handsome but sinister-looking Christopher Lee found — if you will excuse the obvious pun — a part he could sink his teeth into. The film was literally swimming in blood.

Lee's Dracula was younger and better-looking than Lugosi's. He also looked a lot more dangerous. You knew this Dracula could tear your throat out. But he is also less exotic, less mysterious.

Lee's Dracula was so successful that he did several more turns as the vampire count. In one, *Dracula, Prince of Darkness* (1965), Lee plays the character pretty much as he was described in the original novel. In this film, when we first meet Dracula, he is a tall old man with a white moustache. He is dressed all in black. The most impressive scene in the film is not one in which any blood is spilled. It is one in which Dracula talks about the good old days, when his warrior ancestors ruled Transylvania. That whole speech comes right out of the original novel. *Dracula, Prince of Darkness* is the best and most interesting Christopher Lee Dracula film.

It was Christopher Lee's Dracula that really sparked the modern interest in Dracula and vampires in general. Today vampires are the most popular of movie monsters.

A reference book, *The Filmgoer's Companion*, has this to say about Christopher Lee: "Seems to have made more films than any other living actor, and certainly played most of the known monsters."

Lee as the Mummy

Lee himself has objected to that statement. He says he can name two or three actors who have made more films. But he can't possibly deny the second part of the sentence.

In addition to the Frankenstein monster and Dracula, Lee has also played the Mummy, Dr. Jekyll and Mr. Hyde, Rasputin the mad monk, Dr. Fu Manchu, the evil Rochefort in *The Three Musketeers,* and assorted devil worshipers, mad scientists, homicidal maniacs, and other sinister and villainous types. Though he usually plays the bad guy, he has also played Sherlock Holmes.

Christopher Lee has sometimes displayed a fine comic sense. He has been very successful at doing comic vampire and other sinister characters in films and on TV. Even when being funny, Lee has sort of an icy dignity. This keeps him from ever looking like a sad parody of himself. You laugh, but a little nervously. You are never quite sure that he won't come after you, fangs bared.

Recently Christopher Lee has tried to shake the old Dracula image. He has tried to do a wider variety of parts. He even gets a bit irritated with interviewers who ask him about Dracula.

Today actors are not so easily typecast, put in the same kind of role. They have more freedom to choose what roles they will play. But Christopher Lee will never shake Dracula. Why should he? He created a part that was loved by millions. That is, if you can ever love a vampire.

4

VINCENT PRICE –
THE ELEGANT VILLAIN

Americans don't seem to believe that their fellow Americans can be particularly monstrous. Most of the stars of horror films that have become popular in America were born in England. A few were born in Germany or Hungary. Of the major horror film stars, only two were native Americans. The star of silent films, Lon Chaney, was one. Vincent Price is the other.

Price was born in 1911 in St. Louis, Missouri, and graduated from Yale University. But his background is not completely American. After college, he went to school in England where he studied, not acting, but art history. He began his acting career in England. It was only after he became a success there that Vincent Price returned to America, and to Broadway and Hollywood.

His film career began in 1938. He didn't start out playing monsters, but he rarely played heroes. In his best known nonhorror films he played the good-for-nothing Shelby in *Laura* (1944) and the evil Cardinal Richelieu in *The Three Musketeers* (1948).

Vincent Price

Price's first real horror film was *The Tower of London* (1939) in which he was more victim than villain. He took the part of the Invisible Man in *The Invisible Man Returns* (1940). The original *Invisible Man* was a classic and starred Claude Rains. In this sequel, the invisible Price is a hero, not a villain or monster. There is very little horror in the film, though it is often shown in horror film series. *The Invisible Man Returns* doesn't really work. It did little for Price's career in horror films.

Price really began to emerge as a leading star of horror films during the 1950s. Unlike Karloff and Lugosi or Lee, he was not launched by a big film. There is no single horror character with which he is always associated. His reputation was built by making a lot of films.

The closest to a hit horror film that Price ever had was *House of Wax* (1953). It was a 3-D film. It is probably the best 3-D film ever made. Price starred as the horribly scarred and mad sculptor who murders people and turns them into wax dummies. It's not a great horror film, but it is a good one. It is entertaining, even when seen in its "flat" version.

Entertaining is an important word to remember when dealing with Vincent Price. Price is a bit of a ham. He overacts in practically everything he does. And he knows he is overacting. There is usually a touch of humor, a little self-mockery in every Vincent Price horror film. As a result, his films are fun and funny, even when they are frightening. In their best films, Karloff, Lugosi and Lee were never funny.

Price appeared in a number of gimmick horror films

made during the fifties. There were films in which inflated skeletons were lowered into the audience. And there were films where seats were wired to give a mild electric shock. Most of these films have been forgotten. They deserve to be forgotten.

Price didn't always play the villain in horror films either. Take the science fiction–horror film, *The Fly* (1958). *The Fly* is about an unfortunate scientist who gets his molecules mixed up with those of a fly. The result is that the scientist has the head and arm of a fly, and the fly has the head and arm of a scientist. The plot sounds silly, and it is.

Price did not play the scientist/fly. He had a rather unimportant background role. Price said the picture was a hard one to make, because every time he saw the actor in his fly makeup, he burst out laughing. The film company had to keep reshooting the scenes. You can't have one of the actors breaking up, every time the monster appears.

In the sixties, Price entered a new phase of his horror film career. He teamed up with director Roger Corman to do a series of films based on Edgar Allan Poe stories. Poe's stories are not easy to bring to the screen. In fact, sometimes Corman's pictures use little more of Poe than the title. The films were all shot on a very low budget. Price is practically the only "name" actor in any of them. The films usually involve Price in costume, wandering about some gloomy castle or decaying house. They are films about people being locked in rooms, or buried alive, or going stark, raving mad.

Price leers, sneers, grovels, threatens, declaims, and generally acts in the grand manner. And he does it very effectively and entertainingly. The Poe series proved to be extremely popular, particularly among teens.

Though Price normally avoids heavy and grotesque makeup for his roles, he looked quite grotesque in one of his non-Poe films, *The Abominable Dr. Phibes* (1971).

Sometimes there is more than just his usual hint of humor in Price's horror roles. In a couple of the films that he did with Corman, *The Raven* (1963) and *The Comedy of Terrors* (1963), Price was teamed with the likes of Boris Karloff, Peter Lorre, and Basil Rathbone. These were out-and-out spoofs of the horror film.

But *Theatre of Blood* (1973) is a different matter entirely. It's supposed to be a comedy. Price plays a murderous ham actor revenging himself on the critics. The film is funny. But it is also extremely violent. It's not the sort of film you go to see if you are only looking for a laugh. You will get a shudder as well.

There is one little known film in which Price shows that he does not have to overact, and that he does not have to mock himself. The film, released in 1968, was called *The Conqueror Worm* in the United States. It was made in Britain, and there it had the title *Witchfinder General*. It is based on the true story of Matthew Hopkins, a professional witchhunter of the seventeenth century. Hopkins was responsible for the torture and death of hundreds of innocent people accused of witchcraft.

Price plays Hopkins as a brutal, greedy, and corrupt man. His performance is restrained and highly effective.

There isn't a single laugh in the film. *The Conqueror Worm* is a shocking, violent, and depressing film. Many fans of horror films consider it the best film that Vincent Price ever made.

Star of horror films is only one side of the public personality of Vincent Price. He is a man of highly refined tastes. Remember he first studied art history before taking up acting. He is still an expert on art, and he frequently writes and lectures on the subject. He is also a great gourmet cook, and gourmet cooking is another subject that he often writes and lectures on.

When public television presented a highly popular series of British mystery shows called, appropriately enough, "Mystery," Price was chosen as the host of the series.

At other times you can catch him on TV commercials advertising "real dairy products."

All in all, Vincent Price is a most elegant villain.

5

ALSO STARRING I

From Universal Studios, the home of horror in the 1930s and 1940s, came three great monsters. Though some of the films featuring these monsters are nearly fifty years old, the images are still with us today. The monsters are Dracula, the Frankenstein monster, and the Wolf Man. Bela Lugosi was Dracula. Boris Karloff was the Frankenstein monster. Who played the Wolf Man?

The actor who starred as the tormented werewolf in the 1941 classic film *The Wolf Man* bore a famous name, Lon Chaney, Jr. He was the son of the Man of a Thousand Faces, Lon Chaney, star of many great silent horror films. Universal had heavily promoted Lon Chaney, Jr.'s career. He seemed destined for monster superstardom. But Chaney, Jr. never became as famous as his father. Nor did he ever match Karloff and Lugosi in popularity. There is an excellent reason why he fell short. Lon Chaney, Jr. wasn't a very good actor.

He was a big hulking fellow. In his wolf man makeup he looked genuinely frightening. As poor Lawrence Tal-

Lon Chaney in *The Phantom of the Opera*

bot, the unwilling human side of the werewolf, he looked as if he was suffering and tortured. As Talbot, he could groan, and as the Wolf Man, he could growl — and that was it. That was his whole range of emotions.

Lon Chaney, Jr.

No, that's not really fair. Lon Chaney, Jr. appeared in one really notable nonhorror part. It was a film called *Of Mice and Men*. He plays a good but dull-witted migrant laborer. His performance is so touching, it can make you

41

cry. If you get a chance to see that film, please do. You will see the Wolf Man out of makeup, and as a startlingly different character.

In addition to the Wolf Man, Chaney, Jr. took his turn playing the other great horror monsters. He was the Frankenstein monster and the Mummy. All that these parts required is that the actor wear a lot of makeup and stomp around. Neither Chaney, Jr. nor others who followed Karloff in these roles was required to do much acting. Lon Chaney, Jr., was also cast as a suave vampire in *Son of Dracula* (1942). The result was embarrassing. Lon Chaney, Jr. just didn't look right in evening clothes.

Still, he gave us *The Wolf Man*. And for that he will not be forgotten.

I said that there were three Universal Studios monsters of the 1930s and 1940s. I really should have said four. The fourth one was hard to see. He was invisible.

In the early thirties, Universal decided to do a film version of the famous H. G. Wells story, *The Invisible Man*. They wanted to again team up the pair that had made *Frankenstein* such a success: director, James Whale, and star, Boris Karloff. Whale liked the idea. Karloff didn't. He didn't think that his career would be helped much by playing the part. He would be seen only for a brief moment at the end of the film. All the rest of the time, he would just be a figure wrapped in bandages or only a voice. So the studio picked another relatively unknown English actor, Claude Rains.

The real stars of *The Invisible Man* (1933) had to be the highly sophisticated special effects and Whale's di-

Lon Chaney, Jr., as the Wolf Man

rection. The film hovered between horror and humor. But Rains' voice fitted the part perfectly. From the way he talked, you could hear the personality of the invisible Dr. Griffin change from a scientist trapped by his own experiment to a murderous madman.

The Invisible Man was a great success. But it didn't quite make a major horror star out of Claude Rains. There is no reason to believe that Rains had any desire to become identified with a particular type of film. He did play in a couple of other notable horror films. Rains was the werewolf's father in *The Wolf Man*. Rains also starred in the sound and color remake of *The Phantom of the Opera* (1943). In the classic Lon Chaney silent version, and in the original book, the phantom is some sort of a deformed monster. Rains plays the part very differently. He is a violinist who had been horribly scarred by acid. It is a much more human phantom.

Claude Rains in *The Phantom of the Opera*

If you are fans of old movies in general, you will recognize Claude Rains in a nonhorror role. He played the cynical French police chief in *Casablanca* (1942). That famous film also contained a couple of other faces familiar to all horror film fans. Conrad Veidt, who was the star of *The Cabinet of Dr. Caligari, The Man Who Laughs* and other silent horrors, appeared as the evil Nazi commander. Veidt, a German actor who fled the Nazis in the

Conrad Veidt

1930s, played a lot of Nazi parts when he got to Hollywood. The other familiar star of horror films in *Casablanca* was also a refugee from the Nazis. His name was Peter Lorre.

Peter Lorre in *M*

Lorre's real name was Laszlo Löwenstein, and he was born in Hungary. He had been a star in German films, but when the Nazis took over he came to America and to Hollywood. Next to Karloff himself, there is no horror film star that I personally like as much as Peter Lorre.

Lorre was a very small man, with a very round head, eyes like hard-boiled eggs, and a strangely sinister voice. His voice may have been better known than his face. Imitating Lorre's voice, like imitating Karloff's voice, was part of the act of every impressionist of the forties and fifties. Lorre was rarely the monster — he was too small for that part — he was more often the madman.

Lorre's first major film part in Germany was in a film called *M*, in which he played an insane killer of children. In that part, he was both frightening and strangely sympathetic.

In Hollywood he played one of the maddest of all film madmen, Dr. Gogol, in the film *Mad Love* (1935). Lorre giggles and slithers through the part of the loony doctor in high style. In *The Beast With Five Fingers* (1947) he is a madman again, but a more tormented and sympathetic one. Lorre could also play the straight, sinister villain. He did this in Alfred Hitchcock's original *The Man Who Knew Too Much*. Lorre was also marvelously funny and a bit sinister in a nonhorror film you have probably seen, *The Maltese Falcon* (1941). He was Joel Cairo. While Peter Lorre was in a lot of good films, he never really got the parts he deserved.

A lot of horror stars wound up doing comedy. Often they played comic imitations of themselves. Sometimes that was sad. Peter Lorre did a lot of comedy. This was particularly true near the end of his career, when he had gotten very fat. But unlike some of the other horror actors, Lorre had a real gift for comic parts. There was nothing sad or degrading about his performance.

Peter Lorre was more than just a "personality" or a "star." He was an actor, and a good one. That made all the difference in the world.

Basil Rathbone will be forever identified with the role of clever detective Sherlock Holmes. It is a part he often played in a highly successful series of films. These films

Basil Rathbone

often show up on TV today, even though they were made in the 1940s. Rathbone was also Sherlock Holmes on a popular radio series. But he didn't play only the great detective. He also appeared in a lot of horror films during the 1930s and 1940s. The best of them was *Son of Frankenstein* (1939). Rathbone played the son — not the monster's son, Dr. Frankenstein's son. In this film, he is a misunderstood hero rather than a mad scientist.

Rathbone is far more villainous in *The Tower of London* (1939), probably his best horror film. The director of this film was Rowland V. Lee, who had also directed *Son of Frankenstein*. The team of Karloff and Rathbone was very successful in *Son*. Lee hoped to repeat the success with *Tower*. In *Tower*, Rathbone plays the evil Duke of Gloucester, later to become the evil King Richard III. Karloff is his sidekick Mord, the bald, limping executioner. Rathbone is simply wonderful here. He is every bit as sinister as Karloff, and a bit more so.

There is one scene in this film dear to the hearts of all horror film fans. Richard and Mord drown the Duke of Clarence in a large vat of wine. And who plays the Duke of Clarence? A young Vincent Price. Later, when Price became a superstar of horror films, he was in a remake of *The Tower of London*. This time he took Rathbone's old part as Richard III. Price is good, but Basil Rathbone did it better.

Like so many actors, Basil Rathbone ended his career appearing in a lot of trash. Often he played a parody of himself. But *Comedy of Terrors* (1963) is better than junk like *The Ghost in the Invisible Bikini* (1966), one of Karloff's last films. In the first place, *Comedy* was directed by Jacques Tourneur, one of the better directors of horror films.

More importantly, *Comedy of Terrors* was sort of a class reunion for some of the horror film greats. Also appearing were Boris Karloff, Peter Lorre, and Vincent Price. All right, this film about murder among the undertakers isn't great. It may not even be very good. But the actors seem to be having a fine time. And for horror film fans, just watching Rathbone, Price, Lorre, and Karloff enjoy themselves is a lot of fun.

6

ALSO STARRING II

Most of the stars covered in the last chapter had, at one time or another, worked at Universal Studios in Hollywood. During the 1930s and 1940s, Universal was where the best and the most horror films were being made. But by the 1950s, the old Hollywood studio system had begun to break up. Television had made movies less profitable, and a lot of films were being made outside of Hollywood. The new home of horror became Britain's Hammer Studios.

Like Universal, Hammer had a regular group of actors for its horror films. The star was, of course, Christopher Lee. Second in line was Peter Cushing. The team of Lee and Cushing was the most durable in the history of horror films. Cushing played Dr. Frankenstein to Lee's monster. He was the archaeologist while Lee was the Mummy, and Van Helsing when Lee played Dracula. When Lee was Dr. Fu Manchu, Cushing appeared as Nayland Smith, the evil doctor's most persistent enemy.

Cushing has also appeared without Lee in a huge num-

51

Peter Cushing

ber of other horror films. Some, such as *Dr. Terror's House of Horrors* (1964), are pretty good. Others, like *The Beast Must Die* (1979), are perfectly awful. *Beast* starts with a clever idea. It tries to combine horror and whodunit. In the film, one member of a group at a house party is a werewolf. Near the end of the film, the viewer is given a "werewolf break." You are supposed to guess which one of the suspects is the werewolf. Cute. Unfortunately the film is dull. Most of it consists of scenes of people walking through the woods. The wolf looks like (and probably is) a fat German shepherd dog. By the time the "werewolf break" comes along, you don't care who the werewolf is anymore. Most of the time, poor Peter Cushing just stands around looking as confused and bored as the audience must feel.

Peter Cushing is a striking-looking man. In his better films, he shows that he has real ability as an actor. He is able to project an evil dignity that is truly effective. Yet he was never able to reach the top rank of horror film stardom. That special quality that separates the great from the near great is somehow missing in Peter Cushing.

Oliver Reed also starred in Hammer films though he has never been completely identified with horror films. His first major part was as Bill Sykes, in the musical *Oliver*. He has also appeared in so many horror films, and he is so good, that he surely can be classed as a star of horror.

Reed is a big, solid, rather brutal-looking fellow. He is a bit like Lon Chaney, Jr. But there is one big difference. Oliver Reed is a good actor.

Not surprisingly, Reed's first major horror film was a werewolf film, *Curse of the Werewolf* (1961). This was Hammer's werewolf movie. It is better than Universal's original *Wolf Man* film. The film has all the familiar features of Hammer horror. There is vivid color, beautiful backgrounds, and an awful lot of blood and violence. It is a really gruesome film. But it rises above the mere blood-and-guts shocker mainly because of Oliver Reed's performance. He is a powerful man, struggling to keep down the beast within him — and finally losing. The werewolf has never been done better.

Reed has done well in some fairly standard horror films like *Paranoiac* and *Burnt Offerings*. In one he plays the villain, in the other the victim. Reed is also the star of a Canadian-made horror film, *The Brood* (1979). This film, and its director, David Cronenberg, have developed quite a reputation among horror film fans. Reed plays a somewhat mad scientist, Dr. Hal Raglan. He runs an institution for the insane. One of his patients is a woman named Nola. When she really gets angry, she is able to give birth to malformed and murderous children, "the brood." These creatures go around killing everyone Nola is mad at.

Some of the scenes between Oliver Reed, as Dr. Raglan, and Samantha Eggar, as Nola, are so intense that they leave the viewer exhausted. Here is a warning. Even if you have become used to the slice and dice type of horror film, you may not be able to handle *The Brood*.

Through the years there have been several different actors who might be called the king of horror. But there

Oliver Reed in *Curse of the Werewolf*

is only one actress who has ever deserved the title queen of horror. She is Barbara Steele. It's not that there is anything horrible-looking about Barbara Steele. Quite the reverse. She is a remarkably beautiful woman. She has a strange, haunting, and sometimes diabolical sort of beauty.

In most horror films, women have been victims. Steele has usually played the villain. And when she *is* the victim, she is rarely an innocent victim.

Barbara Steele was born in England. Or perhaps it was Ireland. She has told different stories about herself. She started acting on the stage when she was quite young. She made some pictures in Britain during the late 1950s. Then she went to Hollywood, where she was very unhappy. She said she spent most of her time on the beach waiting for the phone to ring. It didn't ring very often.

Steele's career was at a dead end. There was no work for her in America and very little in England. So she went to Italy. There she teamed up with Mario Bava, a photographer turned film director. Bava was to go on to become Italy's top director of horror films. Barbara Steele was to become the sixties' number one horror film star. And she has become a true cult figure, with a devoted following.

It all started in 1960 with *Black Sunday*. The film has also been shown under the titles *Mask of the Demon*, *Revenge of the Vampire* and *House of Fright*. But most often it is called *Black Sunday*.

The plot is fairly complicated. The film begins with Steele playing Asa, a witch executed in 1630. Then she also plays Katia, a descendant of the dead witch. That's

Barbara Steele in *Black Sunday*

not quite right, because Asa isn't really dead. She comes back to a sort of life when her tomb is disturbed. The rest of the film is about the witch's attempt to drink Katia's blood and be restored to full life.

The film is beautifully photographed, but it is very gruesome. It was banned completely in England for eight years. When it is shown on TV, it is still heavily edited. Even now, after scores of violent horror films, *Black Sunday* can jolt you.

In the film, Barbara Steele dies horribly not once, but twice. The first time is when she is executed as a witch in 1630. She has a spiked mask driven into her face. When she is again executed, two hundred years later, she is burned at the stake. Steele gets to do a lot of screaming in this film.

She also gets a chance to display her acting talents by playing two very different characters, the evil Asa and the sweet Katia.

The film was greeted with near hysterical enthusiasm by horror film fans. They praised Steele's beauty and her acting ability. They also found in her a certain mysterious quality which made her not just good in horror films, but great. Her career as the queen of horror was launched.

She also appeared in the *Pit and the Pendulum* (1961), one of director Roger Corman's Edgar Allan Poe adaptations. The star was Vincent Price. She also appeared in *The Crimson Cult* (1970), one of Boris Karloff's last films. It was released after his death. Christopher Lee was also in that one. In spite of the cast, it's not very good.

Most of Steele's horror films were made in Italy. Like *Black Sunday*, they appeared in the U.S. and Britain under an amazing variety of titles. *Castle of Blood* has also been called *Terror, The Long Night of Terror, Tombs of Horror, Coffin of Terror* and *Castle of Terror*. One critic complained that the film has almost more titles than cast members.

Steele has played vengeful ghosts, long-dead sorceresses, vampires, and once in a while, a victim.

Now and again she has also appeared in nonhorror films, usually in very strange parts. In a film called *Caged Heat* (1974), she was a disabled and sadistic warden of a women's prison.

Barbara Steele has had small parts in several major nonhorror films. Most of her work, though, has been done with small, independent producers. She has often complained that she is typecast in horror films. She has said she would like to make a beautiful love film, but has never been given the chance.

In short, Barbara Steele has never been a big star, but she is a thoroughly professional actress. And she has that mysterious quality that inspires fanatic devotion in some film fans. She will be remembered long after many of the "stars" of today have been forgotten.

One of today's stars who will never be forgotten is Bette Davis. She's one of the greatest actresses in film history — truly a legend in her own time. What is she doing in a book about horror films? Let me explain.

Bette Davis had been a major film star since the early 1930s. She had picked up two Academy Awards and had

Bette Davis

been nominated for several more. But by the early 1960s, her great career had hit a low point. She was no longer being offered the best parts.

Then in 1961, director Robert Aldrich asked her if she wanted to be in a film called *What Ever Happened to Baby Jane?* Her costar was to be another great lady of films who had fallen on hard times — Joan Crawford.

Davis was to play a one-time child star, grown old and

crazy. Crawford was to be her sister, who had once been a glamorous movie star, but had been crippled and now used a wheelchair. As Davis goes crazier and crazier, she tries in various horrible ways to kill her disabled sister. There is also a dandy and very surprising turnabout at the end.

Both stars liked the script and both agreed to work for far less than their usual fee. But the big studios were not anxious to put money into Aldrich's project. The studios figured Davis and Crawford were washed up. But Aldrich insisted, and finally a deal was put together.

There were all sorts of rumors about fights between the two stars. The fights may have been real. Or it might have all been publicity — the film got a *lot* of publicity. When it was released, the public lined up to see it. *What Ever Happened to Baby Jane?* was a huge success.

The success gave Bette Davis' career a big lift. In 1964 she did *Hush . . . Hush, Sweet Charlotte.* The film was supposed to bring Crawford and Davis together again. But Joan Crawford became ill. She was replaced by another famed film actress, Olivia De Havilland. Davis plays a mad and murderous aging southern belle.

A lot of people were disappointed that Joan Crawford wasn't in *Hush . . . Hush Sweet Charlotte.* But in general, people were very impressed with the film, particularly with Bette Davis.

Next, it was off to England for *The Nanny* (1965). Davis was somewhat less mad this time, but equally murderous. She also appeared in *Burnt Offerings* with Oliver Reed. In this film, she doesn't have a lot to do.

Throughout the seventies, Bette Davis appeared in several made-for-TV movies. She was the evil mastermind in *Madame Sin* (1972) and the mother of a sculptor obsessed with evil in *Scream, Pretty Peggy* (1974). She was the head of a deadly secret cult in *The Dark Secret of Harvest Home* (1978). None of these made-for-TV films is particularly good. But even in a second-rate film, Bette Davis is worth watching.

After the great success of *Baby Jane,* Joan Crawford too began showing up in a succession of horror films. The goriest was *Straitjacket* (1964). The ads warned "*Straitjacket* vividly depicts ax murders." It sure does. It's the sort of picture that can shock you without really scaring you. And in the end, you get bored with it.

In 1969, Crawford was the star of the opening segment of a TV series called *Night Gallery.* The series had been conceived and written by Rod Serling. But the actual direction of the show was done by a nineteen-year-old on his first real directing job. The young man's name was Steven Spielberg. Sound familiar? Spielberg was to go on to become one of the most successful directors in the history of films. Among his films are *Jaws, Close Encounters of the Third Kind, Raiders of the Lost Ark* and *E.T.* But his very first job was directing Joan Crawford in a TV horror show. Crawford had the reputation of being a tough actress to direct. Spielberg said at first he was scared to death. He said that she had some trouble memorizing the lines, but otherwise, she wasn't that hard to work with.

Joan Crawford died on May 10, 1977. After her death,

her daughter wrote a book about her called *Mommie Dearest*. It later was made into a successful film. In the book and film, Joan Crawford was depicted as something of a human monster. But no matter what she may have been personally — she was one fine actress.

Then there is Ray Milland. He is not specifically known for his roles in horror films. During the thirties and forties, he was a popular leading man and later a character actor. He did, however, star in *The Uninvited* (1944). This film is one of the two or three best pure ghost stories ever filmed. It's funny, romantic and frightening all at once. If you like ghost stories, you'll love *The Uninvited*.

Later Milland began appearing in a lot of low-budget horror films. He had the distinction of appearing in two of the worst horror films ever made. One was *Frogs* (1972). Here Milland has to fight off attacks by a gang of murderous frogs, yes, frogs.

The same year he made an even worse film, *The Thing With Two Heads*. Milland plays a mad doctor who hates blacks. The doctor also is dying of cancer. He decides to have his head removed from his disease-ridden body and placed on a healthy body. The body belongs to Rosie Grier, a former football player, and a black man.

Throughout much of the film, Grier runs around with a rather poor model of Milland's head attached to one of his broad shoulders. Unless you have seen this one, you cannot believe how silly it is.

Both *Frogs* and *The Thing With Two Heads* are so bad, they are treasured by people who love really bad movies.

7

the victims

If you have a monster or a villain, you must also have a victim. The victim in the horror film is almost always a woman. It isn't that the monsters don't kill men. They wipe out scores of males. A really good monster can stomp out a whole village. But in the end, it always comes down to the scene where the monster or villain menaces the girl.

The first real victim of this type was Lili Dagover, a German film actress. She has to be considered the first because she appeared in the first real horror film, *The Cabinet of Dr. Caligari.* There is a scene where she is carried off by Conrad Veidt, who plays the evil "sleep-walker." This film was made in 1920. Dagover came to Hollywood in the twenties, but she never made a career of horror films.

All that Lili Dagover had to do in her films was look pale and faint a lot. Another German actress, Birgitte Helm, really had to act. She was the female lead in the classic film called *Metropolis* made in 1926. Helm was only sixteen when she was picked by director Fritz Lang. In *Metropolis*, she, a lovely young girl, is kidnapped and replaced by a robot duplicate. Helm naturally played both parts. She is very effective both as the good Maria and her evil robot double. Helm went on to star as the victim, or sometimes the villain, in a number of other German films. Although prints of most of her films were lost during World War II, *Metropolis* remains. That single film is enough to establish her reputation as a heroine of the horrors.

The queen of the silent horror film in America was Mary Philbin. She starred with Lon Chaney in the original film of *The Phantom of the Opera* (1925). The moment when she rips the mask from the face of the phantom is one of the most memorable in the history of horror films.

She starred with Conrad Veidt in the grotesque horror film *The Man Who Laughs* (1928). She was with Veidt again in *The Last Performance* (1929). He plays an evil hypnotist and she his helpless victim. Mary Philbin made a lot of films, but the only one that she is really remembered for is *Phantom*.

In the field of victims in horror films, there is one name which towers above all the rest. She reached the greatest heights, the pinnacle of her profession — she reached the top of the Empire State Building in the palm of a giant ape. I am referring, of course, to Fay Wray, the girl of King Kong's dreams.

Fay Wray — her real name — went to Hollywood High School. Almost immediately after graduation, she began

Fay Wray

working as a film extra. By the time *Kong* came along, she already had a well-established film career. She was not a star, but she worked steadily in different sorts of films. These included musicals, comedies, costume dramas, and some horror films. Even before *King*, she had played victim to villainous Lionel Atwill in such films as *Doctor X, The Vampire Bat,* and *The Mystery of the Wax Museum.* Though the films were all made in the early 1930s, they are quite "watchable" today.

But it was *King Kong* that made Fay Wray immortal. Ask anyone who the human star of *King Kong* was. The first name that nine out of ten people will come up with is Fay Wray. *King Kong* is one of the very few horror films in which the victim was the star. Quickly now, who was the female lead in the original *Dracula* and in the original *Frankenstein?* I'll bet you can't remember without looking it up.

Fay Wray has been hailed by critics of horror films as "a great screamer." Some of her terror may have been real. In most scenes, the "giant" gorilla was really an eighteen-inch-high model. Trick photography was used to make it look huge. But there were scenes in which the gorilla was supposed to hold Fay Wray in its hand. Trick photography wouldn't work. An eight-foot-long mechanical hairy hand and arm were constructed. The device lifted her about ten feet off the ground. But when the arm went up, the hand's grip would loosen.

"My fear was real," Fay Wray recalled. "I grabbed onto his wrist, his thumb, whatever I could to keep from slipping out of that paw!"

Three months after *Kong* opened to huge and enthusiastic audiences, Fay Wray was off shooting *Below the Sea*. In this film, she was menaced by a giant mechanical squid.

Fay Wray continued to make movies throughout the 1930s, 1940s and 1950s. Most of these were detective films or light romantic comedies. She never specialized in horror after *King Kong*. Her voice became familiar to millions of radio listeners, for she appeared frequently on radio dramas. When television began, Fay Wray was there too. She was in dramas and series like *Alfred Hitchcock Presents* and *The Perry Mason Show*. She even co-authored a play with the great American novelist Sinclair Lewis.

By the mid-1960s "the great screamer" had pretty much retired from acting. Hers had been a long and successful career. But as she often said, her entire life would be shadowed by that giant ape. And her fame has been passed on through her family. Her daughter Victoria appeared in a TV commercial for the candy bar Almond Joy. In the commercial she is asked why an Almond Joy comes in two pieces. "So I can share it," she says. "There's a piece for me and a piece for my friend." At that moment, a giant hairy hand reaches through the window and gently takes one half of the candy bar.

A moment ago, I asked about the female leads in *Dracula* and *Frankenstein*. In *Dracula* it was Helen Chandler. In *Frankenstein* it was Mae Clark. Both were well-known actresses before they appeared with the great monsters. When the films were originally released, both were given star billing. Who remembers them now?

If you are an old film buff, you might remember Mae Clark, but not from a horror film. Before *Frankenstein*, she played a string of tough-girl roles. Shortly before *Frankenstein*, she appeared in the film *The Public Enemy*, with James Cagney. In one famous scene, Cagney squashes a grapefruit in her face. The monster was more of a gentleman.

If you somehow run across a science fiction serial called *King of the Rocket Men*, the actress playing Glendy, the spunky photographer from *Miracle Science* magazine, may look faintly familiar. It's Mae Clark.

During the 1950s, Hollywood produced a whole string of mildly horrific science fiction films. As you might expect, the girl is still being menaced by the monster. In these films, the monster usually comes from outer space. A lot of actresses were menaced by otherworldly creatures — but none more often than Faith Domergue.

It wasn't supposed to be that way. Faith Domergue was supposed to be a big star. She had attracted the attention of Howard Hughes, the eccentric billionaire who sometimes produced movies. Hughes' money had propelled other actresses into stardom. He intended to do the same with Faith. He spent over $3 million promoting her. But somehow it never worked. The film that was supposed to launch her career ran into endless production problems. When it was finally released, it was a dud.

Domergue had to settle for a less glamorous acting

career. She did a lot of television. She also made some unmemorable films — and one that is still considered a classic. The film is *This Island Earth* (1954). Domergue plays Ruth Adams, a beautiful nuclear physicist.

During the 1930s and 1940s the victims in most horror films were usually innocent bystanders. They attracted the monster's attention because of their beauty. In the science fiction horror films of the fifties, the victims were often beautiful scientists. But like their less educated sisters of earlier times, they too screamed, fainted, and were carried off. In *This Island Earth*, the menacing monster is a real fright. It is a half-human, half-insect thing called a mutant.

In 1955 Domergue was being menaced by a really huge octopus in *It Came From Beneath the Sea*. (Yes, I know that sounds like the film Fay Wray appeared in twenty years earlier.) That same year, Domergue appeared in a more traditional horror film, *Cult of the Cobra*. This time she plays a villain, not a victim. She is Lisa, the vengeful member of a snake cult, who can actually change herself into a snake. But she was back to being a victim again in another sci-fi thriller, *The Atomic Man*.

That was in 1956, and by that time the entire movie industry was reeling under the impact of television. So Faith Domergue took her talents to the small screen. Then in 1972, she returned to horror films in a low-budget vehicle *The House of the Seven Corpses*.

No one could claim that Faith Domergue was a great, or even a particularly good, actress. She had a flat style of acting that somehow typifies the films of the 1950s. She has a loyal following. In fact, there is still a virtual Faith Domergue cult. Next time *This Island Earth* or *It Came From Beneath the Sea* shows up on the *Late, Late Show,* look around your neighborhood. See who still has their lights on and is watching TV. There may be a Faith Domergue cultist in there.

The Hammer horrors of the late fifties featured a regular group of performers. They starred Christopher Lee and Peter Cushing, as monster and scientist. Who was the victim? Often it was Hazel Court. She played Elizabeth, the cousin Dr. Frankenstein is engaged to marry, in *The Curse of Frankenstein* (1957). Another Hammer horror epic, *The Man Who Could Cheat Death* (1959), has Court as the potential victim of a mad 104-year-old scientist. He is kept young by gland transplants. In the climactic scene, he suffers a sudden attack of old age and begins to decay before Court's horrified eyes. One oddity of this film is that the good guy is played by the usually villainous Christopher Lee. In a third Hammer film, *Dr. Blood's Coffin* (1961), Court again finds herself in the clutches of a mad doctor.

Court then went on to work with director Roger Corman in some of his very best horror films. She starred in *The Masque of the Red Death* (1964). Her costar was Vincent Price. In *The Premature Burial* (1962), she is Ray Milland's evil wife. She manages to drive her husband mad. A little too mad, as it turns out, because Milland carries her off screaming and buries her alive.

Adrienne Barbeau

The Raven (1963) was a Corman horror satire. It tries to make fun of horror films as a whole. Boris Karloff, Peter Lorre, and Vincent Price are all in it doing comic exaggerations of their usual horror roles. Hazel Court is right in there with them. She is in some pretty fast company. But she showed that she could act and clown around with the best of them. Hazel Court probably deserved better roles than she ever got.

The Fog is a rather silly but enjoyable horror film released in 1980. Horror film fans will continue to see it for years. Not because it's great, but because it has performances by two of the great victims of modern horror films, Adrienne Barbeau and Jamie Lee Curtis. And it has a first-rate performance by one of the great victims of the past, Janet Leigh.

Adrienne Barbeau also starred in *Creepshow* (1982) and *The Swamp Thing* (1981). She's not a bad actress. But in most films she doesn't seem to have much to do, except to stand around and look sexy. That she does very well.

Jamie Lee Curtis is a more interesting character. She has become a real cult figure of modern horror films. She is also the daughter of the actress Janet Leigh. It was Janet Leigh who was hacked up in the shower in the famous Alfred Hitchcock movie *Psycho* (1960). Mother and daughter both appear in *The Fog*.

Curtis is pursued by the ghosts of some angry lepers in *The Fog*. But they are downright friendly, when compared to the menace she faced in *Halloween*, the film that made her famous. This 1978 film is considered one of the scariest films made since *Psycho*.

Jamie Lee Curtis

In *Halloween* Curtis plays Laura, a teen-aged girl pursued by a murderous loon named Michael. Michael is not your ordinary homicidal maniac either. He can be shot and stabbed, and he still keeps coming. In fact he has come back for several sequels, as has Laura. Michael stabs, hacks, impales, boils or otherwise disposes of several boys and girls on his way to Laura. But in the end Laura gets away — barely.

There is a lot more graphic violence in *Halloween* and its sequels and imitators, than in the classic horror films of the thirties and forties. Laura not only screams, she bleeds. But there is another difference. Unlike the victim in the old horror films, Laura fights back. She doesn't just collapse and wait for some man to rescue her. In *Halloween* she stabs Michael. In *Halloween II* she puts long needles through his eyes. Of course, he keeps coming. But she shows a lot of spunk.

Nothing illustrates the difference between the old, passive female victim of the horrors, and the new, more active ones, than the fine 1978 sci-fi horror film *Alien*. In this film, the heroine, played by Sigourney Weaver, not only fights back against a really horrifying monster — she wins. All the men are killed, but she manages to blast the thing out into space.

Monsters of the future, watch out!

Dwight Frye

8

che supporcing casc

Everyone has his or her own favorite scene in horror films. Mine is in the original *Dracula*. It's one in which the vampire count doesn't even appear.

The ship carrying Count Dracula to England has run aground in a storm. The authorities go on board to investigate. The crew is either missing or dead. Then the searchers hear a noise down below. They throw open the hatch door, and up from the depths, grinning and giggling, comes Renfield, now mad as a hatter. It's a great moment.

Renfield was played by Dwight Frye. Frye also gave a memorable performance as Fritz, the hunchbacked assistant, in *Frankenstein*. And he played Karl, Dr. Praetorious' assistant, in *Bride of Frankenstein*. He appeared as the mad doctor's assistant once again in *Frankenstein Meets the Wolf Man*. For a while, Frye dominated the crazed-assistant role in the way that Karloff dominated the monster and mad doctor roles.

Frye was one of a small number of actors who made a

career of supporting parts in horror films. Sometimes the part that such actors created was more memorable than the larger role played by the star. In this chapter, we are going to pay tribute to some of the supporting cast and the characters they created.

During the 1930s, 1940s, and even 1950s, many Hollywood actors worked under contract to a single studio. They didn't have the right to accept or reject parts. If the studio said do this part, they did it, whether they liked it or not. As a result, many actors and actresses found themselves typecast. This means they were playing the same sort of role over and over again. It happened to stars like Karloff and Lugosi. It happened even more often to the members of the supporting cast.

If Dwight Frye was the crazed assistant of the classic horror films, Edward Van Sloan was the good — as opposed to the mad — scientist. He was Van Helsing, the evil count's formidable opponent, in the original *Dracula*. Universal Studios liked his performance so much that they brought him back the following year as Dr. Waldman, Henry Frankenstein's old teacher. In *The Mummy* he was Dr. Muller, an authority on the occult who becomes the evil mummy's most formidable opponent. He returned as the vampire killer in *Dracula's Daughter* (1936). This was Universal's much awaited sequel to the original *Dracula*. The film is often ignored today, probably because it doesn't have any big name stars. But it is a very good film, and grab any chance you get to see it.

Van Sloan's trademark was that he played a scientist

who took the occult and the supernatural seriously. Though the scientist did not necessarily approve of dabbling in such things, he did not scoff at them. That is why he was frequently able to combat the evil. His war cry was "We must find it, and destroy it!"

A common character in most parodies of *Frankenstein* is the wooden-armed German police chief. But there is no character like that in the Mary Shelley novel or the original *Frankenstein* film. Nor does the character appear in *Bride of Frankenstein*. The wooden-armed Inspector Kroegh does not show up until *Son of Frankenstein* — the third of the Frankenstein pictures. The part was played by British-born stage actor Lionel Atwill. He repeated the role in other *Frankenstein* films.

Early in his career, Atwill had been handsome enough to play leading men. By the time he reached Hollywood in 1932, he had begun to specialize in character parts. He played a lot of Germanic types, like that of Inspector Kroegh, and a lot of mad scientists in films like *Murders in the Zoo* and *The Gorilla*. Perhaps his best part, even better than that of Inspector Kroegh, was as the hideously scarred sculptor in the original *Mystery of the Wax Museum*. In the remake, *House of Wax*, that part was taken by Vincent Price — but most agree that Atwill was more frightening. He didn't look like he was kidding.

Sometimes an actor's or actress's entire career will be completely dominated by a single brief role. That's what happened to the British-born actress Elsa Lanchester. She began earning her living as a dancer when she was about fifteen. She has appeared on the stage, in film, in night-

Lionel Atwill

clubs and on TV in a career that has spanned sixty years. She was married to Charles Laughton, one of the world's truly great film and stage actors. Basically, she considers herself a comedienne. But what is she remembered for? A five-minute appearance in *The Bride of Frankenstein*. She was the bride. She was meant to be the *monster's* bride, a female monster. Frankenstein (the scientist) also had a bride, played by Valerie Hobson, but nobody remembers her. Everybody remembers Elsa Lanchester in the streaked fright wig. She was on the screen for a single brief scene. Forty years later she complained that children still recognized her in the supermarket and pointed her out as "Frankenstein's bride." She has, from time to time, appeared in a few other horror films like *Willard* (1971). But it is *The Bride of Frankenstein* that she will always be known for, whether she likes it or not.

Bride really is a marvelous film. Not only does it contain what may have been the best single interpretation of the monster ever. It also has Lanchester's great performance. And it has yet another gemlike supporting part — Dr. Praetorious, played by Ernest Thesiger. In truth the Praetorious part is just sort of stuck in. The part was originally supposed to go to Claude Rains, but he turned it down. So director James Whale called on his old friend Ernest Thesiger.

Thesiger, an amazingly thin and angular actor, is splendid as the power-crazed scientist. Thesiger also appeared in a couple of other Karloff classics from the thirties, *The Old Dark House* and *The Ghoul*. He is always worth watching.

Elsa Lanchester in *The Bride of Frankenstein*

And now a few words about the forgotten man of the *Frankenstein* series. Do you know who played Frankenstein in the original and in *Bride*? No, it was not Boris Karloff — Karloff played the monster. The good doctor himself was played by Colin Clive, another Englishman. Clive played Henry Frankenstein in both. By the way, in the original novel the name of the monster-maker was Victor Frankenstein. For some reason Universal changed the name to Henry. In later *Frankenstein* films, the name reverted to Victor.

Anyway, Colin Clive gives a nice hysterical performance in both films. As I said in chapter 1, he was supposed to be the star of the film. The public thought differently and made Karloff the star. But Colin Clive should not be forgotten, though. He appeared in one other horror classic, *Mad Love* (1935). He gives an even more wonderfully hysterical performance than in the two *Frankensteins*. This time he is a pianist who has been given the hands of an insane knife thrower. The hands insist on doing their own thing, no matter what the rest of the body wants.

From *Frankenstein* let's go to *The Wolf Man*. You doubtless recall these lines from the film.

> *Even a man who is pure at heart,*
> *And says his prayers at night,*
> *Can become a wolf when the wolfbane*
> *   blooms,*
> *And the moon is full and bright.*

They were said by the old gypsy lady whose son happened to be a werewolf. That part was played by the tiny Russian-born actress Maria Ouspenskaya. It is another of those cases when a single role dominates the memory of a whole career. Ouspenskaya was an international stage star before she came to America late in her career. She could not speak a word of English until she was over fifty. And she always spoke with a heavy accent. But in the 1930s and 1940s, Hollywood was where actors from all over the world were going. They went there for a simple reason. Hollywood was where the money was. She appeared in lots of films that no one seems to remember anymore. But everyone remembers her brief role in *The Wolf Man*. It was so good that she repeated the role in *Frankenstein Meets the Wolf Man* (1943).

If Elsa Lanchester and Maria Ouspenskaya are known for single horror film roles, John Carradine is known for playing so many horror film roles. Carradine has appeared in well over two hundred films, perhaps more than any other working actor. He has almost certainly appeared in more horror films. Maybe you don't remember what films you have seen him in, but his tall, gaunt figure and deep voice are instantly recognizable to any horror film fan.

He appeared briefly in *Bride of Frankenstein*, made in 1935, and he was the crazy old man brooding by the fire in the modern werewolf film *The Howling* made in 1981. And he has been just about everything in between including a rather anemic Dracula in *House of Franken-*

stein and *House of Dracula.* He also played the wife-murderer Bluebeard in the film of that name. It was one of his rare starring roles. When I go to see a horror film made anywhere from the mid-thirties to the present day, I always see if I can spot John Carradine. He's usually in there somewhere. His most celebrated role was in a classic nonhorror film, *The Grapes of Wrath.* He played a wandering preacher, and he played the part beautifully.

Once I thought that I was going to have a chance to see Carradine in person. He appeared in a lavish Broadway production of *Frankenstein.* He was the blind old man who befriended the monster. But alas, the show closed after only one performance. The critics hated it. They all agreed that the best thing about the Broadway *Frankenstein* was the appearance of good old John Carradine.

A couple of other familiar faces in horror films, whose names you might not recognize, are J. Carrol Naish and George Zucco. Naish was an Irish-American actor who, in the 1930s and 1940s, specialized in "foreign" parts. He played Italians and Spaniards and Asians — practically anything but an Irishman or an American. In horror films, he is best known for his role as Daniel, the crazed, hunchbacked assistant in *The House of Frankenstein.* That was the old Dwight Frye role. He also had a semi-comic role in *The Beast With Five Fingers.* Naish was in many, many more films.

Zucco was also in *The House of Frankenstein,* as the minor character Professor Lampini. He is murdered by J. Carrol Naish early in the film. But Zucco is better known

George Zucco

for his role as the high priest in a couple of the later mummy films. And he too appeared in scores of horror films from the late thirties through the late fifties.

There they are. Some of the supporting cast. They were never stars. But their performances helped make memorable those films we all enjoy. Next time you sit up past midnight watching the rerun of an old horror film on TV, look closely. You may find yourself saying, "Oh, I recognize him, isn't that . . ."

9

GREAT PERFORMANCES

Every year the Motion Picture Academy gives out awards for all sorts of accomplishments in the movie industry. I would like to suggest a new Academy Award. It might be introduced this way: "Now the award for the best performance in a horror film by an actor or actress not usually associated with horror films. The envelope, please?"

Seriously though, there are a lot of people who have appeared in horror films who never are mentioned in books on horror films. It is because they have only appeared in one or two such films. Yet they have given us great and terrifying moments. Here, we will take a look at some of those great performances.

Any listing of performers of this kind has to be based on personal preference. And personally, one of my favorite actresses of all time is Julie Harris. She's not merely a good actress. She is a great one. One of the greatest of modern times. She has never been a movie star, though she has been in lots of movies. She is probably better known for her work on stage.

What has she done for horror films? She appeared in *The Haunting* (1963). This really fine film is too often neglected. There is no blood and gore. There are not even any ghosts that you see. But if you sit quietly and watch *The Haunting*, it will scare the pants off you.

There are some pretty good special effects in *The Haunting*. And there is plenty of spooky music. But best of all is the performance of Julie Harris. She is a lonely, frightened woman slowly being possessed by the evil of the house. Hers is a completely convincing, completely chilling performance.

Another of my favorite actresses is Sissy Spacek. Her great contribution to horror films is *Carrie* (1976). She played the title role of the unhappy but extremely dangerous Carrie White. And while we are passing out praise for this film, how about a cheer for Piper Laurie? She played Carrie's mad-as-a-hatter mother. Both actresses got Academy Award nominations for their performances. Both deserved the nominations, and both probably deserved the awards.

Ah, yes, Academy Awards. That's a sore point with horror film fans. The nominations for Spacek and Laurie are unusual. Those who appear in horror films are rarely even nominated. And only one has ever won an Oscar.

The sole winner was Fredric March for his portrayal of Dr. Jekyll and Mr. Hyde in the 1932 film version of the famous story by Robert Louis Stevenson. Even then, March had to share his award with Wallace Beery for *The Champ*.

The 1932 *Jekyll and Hyde* is rarely shown. I have only

Fredric March in *Dr. Jekyll and Mr. Hyde*

seen brief clips from it. But in the opinion of those who have seen the film, and who should know, March's performance is one of the most accomplished in film history. Not horror film history — *all* film history. That's saying a great deal.

A lot of famous actors have tried the role of Jekyll and Hyde. When John Barrymore tried it sixty years ago, he was considered America's leading actor. Barrymore gained his fame mainly on the stage. But with the growth of the film industry, he was lured to Hollywood. He first became a star of silent films and later of sound films.

Barrymore was an actor in the grand style. He liked to

John Barrymore (right) in *Dr. Jekyll and Mr. Hyde*

throw his arms about and roll his eyes. This style of
acting was first developed for the stage, where there are
no closeups, no large screen. A person sitting way up in
the balcony had to be able to see what was going on. It is
not a style of acting we are used to today. Even on the
stage, actors today use more restrained gestures and
expressions. Barrymore's performances on film often
look funny to us. But we have to remember that he was
the most popular actor of his time. And his acting skills

were remarkable. Nowhere can that be seen more clearly than in a horror movie.

Dr. Jekyll and Mr. Hyde was one of Barrymore's favorite stage roles. He also did the role on the screen in 1920. What makes this performance so interesting — and really great — is how Barrymore handles the scene when Dr. Jekyll first drinks the potion and changes into Mr. Hyde. That is always the high point of any Jekyll and Hyde performance.

In most filmed versions of the story, heavy makeup and trick photography are used in this scene. But Barrymore had already done the part on the stage. In the theater, you can't stop the cameras and wait for the actor to put on his makeup. Barrymore did the change on film just the way he did it on stage. There is no trick photography, and amazingly enough, no makeup. He does it by drastically changing his expression and posture. It works, it really works. It works so well that the first time you see the Barrymore version of Jekyll and Hyde you will swear that some form of trick photography was involved. The only tricks Barrymore used were the age-old tricks of the actor. The facial change was even tougher on film than on stage because the camera is so close. In these days of special effects, we sometimes forget how much can be done without them.

Barrymore was also very good in the film *Svengali* (1931). He was the evil hypnotist. He did a lot of eye rolling in that one.

Another fine actor who took his turn at Jekyll and Hyde was Spencer Tracy. He did it in a 1941 remake of the film. Like Barrymore, Tracy depended heavily on facial expression in the change from the good doctor to the evil Mr. Hyde. But there was some makeup and trick photography involved as well. Tracy was always a very restrained actor. Some critics have complained that when he played the evil Hyde, he was a bit too restrained. They prefer the theatrics of Barrymore, or the hysterics of March. No slight intended against the other two, but I liked Spencer Tracy. His Hyde was frightening mainly because it was restrained. He seemed very real. He was some evil character that you just might meet — but never wanted to.

People might disagree about Spencer Tracy. But everyone agrees about the greatness of one performance in that film. That was the performance of Ingrid Bergman. She plays Ivy, the poor woman who is tormented to death by Mr. Hyde. In all horror film history, there may never have been a more pathetic and appealing victim of an evil villain. While Ingrid Bergman may be better known for other films, this may have been her finest performance.

For some reason, the name actors identified with horror films have usually stayed away from the Jekyll and Hyde part. There is one exception — Boris Karloff. And he played it strictly for laughs. It was in *Abbott and Costello Meet Dr. Jekyll and Mr. Hyde* (1953). It was one of a series of horror film parodies starring the comedy pair of Bud Abbott and Lou Costello. For the Mr. Hyde parts, Karloff put on a rubber mask, which made him look a lot like the Wolf Man. The film is funny, and it could be scary to young children. But there are no gold stars to be handed out for performances in this one.

The great English actor Charles Laughton gets several gold stars for his work in horror films. His first part in an American film was in that classic tale of people trapped in a spooky house, *The Old Dark House.* He was a good deal more sinister in *The Island of Lost Souls* (1933). The film is based on the H. G. Wells story *The Island of Dr. Moreau.*

Laughton plays Dr. Moreau, a mad scientist. Moreau has been driven from civilization and must perform his experiments on a remote island. What Dr. Moreau is trying to do is turn animals into semihumans. That's why he had been driven from civilization. In the end, the poor creatures revolt against him and drag him off. They clearly are going to perform some sort of horrible experiment on him.

Laughton is quite good as the mad Moreau. The film, however, was considered too horrible and in bad taste by the critics. H. G. Wells denounced it. It was banned entirely in England, and it was not shown widely in the U.S. It's hard to locate the film even today. If you see it, you won't find it very shocking.

Laughton's best performance in a horror film was as the hunchback in *The Hunchback of Notre Dame* (1939). The story should be a familiar one. It is about Quasimodo, the deformed bell ringer, who saves a girl from hanging. And in the end he gives his life for her. The story had been filmed before. In 1923, there was a popular silent version starring Lon Chaney.

Charles Laughton

It has been argued that *The Hunchback of Notre Dame* is not really a horror film. There is nothing supernatural about it. Quasimodo is deformed, but fully human. And he is not a monster, he is very sympathetic. But the Frankenstein monster is sympathetic too. And the final scene with Quasimodo in the tower, while the mob below howls for his blood, is a standard part of many horror films. Then there is also the makeup. Both Chaney and Laughton looked a lot worse as Quasimodo than Karloff did as the Frankenstein monster. You could never convince any kid who had wandered into a showing of *The Hunchback of Notre Dame* that he was not seeing a horror film.

Laughton's Quasimodo is less grotesque than Chaney's. But his portrayal was splendid nevertheless.

Fine acting has not been one of the trademarks of the recent series of slice and dice films. They depend more on shock and blood. But there is one actor that should be singled out. He is Donald Pleasance, the somewhat screwy doctor in *Halloween* and *Halloween II*. Pleasance gives a performance nicely balanced between hysteria and humor. He provides a welcome relief in these tension-filled films.

If I am asked what is my single favorite horror film, I can answer without hesitation. It's *Dead of Night*, a British film made in 1945. The film is really a collection of five short sequences. Each one is a story of the supernatural told by a guest at a British country house. All the stories are separate, yet they are tied together by the end of the film. Almost everyone who knows anything about horror or supernatural films considers *Dead of Night* a classic. It often shows up on TV. In case you haven't seen it, I'm not going to reveal how the stories are tied together. That will spoil it for you. I also suggest that you see this picture from the very beginning or you will miss something important. Those of you who have seen *Dead of Night* know what I'm talking about. The rest of you are in for a real treat and a real scare.

None of the actors in the cast of *Dead of Night* were ever closely associated with horror films. And only one of them was ever even moderately well known in the U.S. He is Michael Redgrave. And it is to Redgrave's performance in this film that I would like to give special mention.

He plays a ventriloquist slowly being taken over by his dummy. The same sort of theme was used in the film *Magic* (1982) starring Anthony Hopkins. *Magic* wasn't bad. In fact it was good. *Dead of Night* was just much much better. In the final scene of the ventriloquist sequence, Redgrave, the ventriloquist, has been put in a mental hospital. He is unable to speak or even move. In order to get him to "snap out of it," the doctors have him visited by a man he tried to kill.

The man enters the room and says hello. Redgrave's dull eyes suddenly brighten. They begin to glitter insanely. His jaw moves mechanically. And then he speaks — in the voice of his dummy — "Hello, Sylvester, I've been waiting for you!"

Michael Redgrave

I was about fourteen years old when I first saw *Dead of Night*. When Redgrave began to speak in that horrible high voice, I slid right out of the theater seat, onto the floor, and covered my ears. I had never been so frightened by a film in all my life.

When you see the film, you may not have quite as strong a reaction as I did. But if you don't at least get an uncontrollable cold shiver, check your pulse. *You* may be dead.

10

OFF-CAMERA STARS

It takes a lot of people to make a horror film, or any film for that matter. There are writers, producers, directors, and cameramen. Some of the people who operate off-camera are as important, or more important, than the actors and actresses who appear on the screen. We are going to take a look at some of these masters of horror.

The greatest monsters of films were invented long before there were any films. Mary Shelley wrote the novel *Frankenstein* in 1816. She was only eighteen years old at the time.

At the start of the film *Bride of Frankenstein*, there is a scene about how the idea of Frankenstein began. In the scene, Mary Shelley, her husband (the poet Percy Shelley) and another poet, Lord Byron, are sitting around telling ghost stories. Mary tells the story of Frankenstein. And that is pretty much how it actually happened.

In 1816 the real Mary Shelley, her husband, and some of their friends were spending the summer in Switzerland. One rainy evening they decided to sit around and

Mary Shelley, author of the novel *Frankenstein*

tell ghost stories. Mary's contribution was a story about a scientist who made an artificial man out of parts of dead bodies. Later that year, she expanded the idea into a full-length book.

Dracula was the creation of (Abraham) Bram Stoker. For thirty years, Stoker was the personal secretary of the great English actor Sir Henry Irving. In his spare time, Stoker wrote novels. Most of them have been forgotten, *Dracula* has not. It can be read with pleasure even today.

Dracula was published in 1897. Stoker's mother wrote him a letter. She thought the book was splendid, "a thousand miles beyond anything you have written before." She said it was the best terror novel since "Mrs. Shelley's *Frankenstein*." That was a mother's pride, but she was right.

Almost everyone agrees that the greatest of all writers of horror stories was Edgar Allan Poe (1809–1849). Poe's stories have probably been used as the basis for more horror movies than the works of any other writer. But as I have already said, Poe's stories are hard to bring to the screen. They are very short. And they rely more on atmosphere than plot. Usually, the screen adaptations of Poe are not very close to the original. The film producers take a title, and perhaps a general idea. Then they add anything they want. The best adaptation of Poe to the screen is *Tales of Terror* (1962). It is a collection of short episodes based on Poe stories. A single Poe story is hard to sustain over a full-length film.

Poe really did write "tales of terror." He didn't write ghost or supernatural stories. Most of his stories are psychological — they are about people who were going mad. Or they rely on sheer physical terror — being buried alive, or slashed to ribbons by a razor-sharp pendulum.

The modern writer considered to be the master of hor-

Edgar Allan Poe, whose stories have been used as the basis of many horror films

ror is Stephen King. His 1975 novel *Carrie* was very popular, and two years later it was made into an even more popular film. That film helped to establish Stephen King as the country's number one writer of horror. Another of King's novels, *The Shining*, was also made into a major film in 1981. It was directed by Stanley Kubrick, who is considered by many to be one of the best directors in the world today.

Stephen King, modern master of horror stories

A lot of horror fans were disappointed with *The Shining*. They found it confusing. And despite the fact that it contains some scenes that will make anyone jump, they found it not quite horrible enough. Personally, I loved it. I think it is one of the very best horror films in recent years. And I think it will last. But only time will tell.

King's long vampire novel, *Salem's Lot*, was made into a long TV film. A bit too long. It was shown over two nights, and, of course, each evening's episode was interrupted by regular commercial breaks. Those are great handicaps for a horror film, since the film depends on building tension. If the viewer is continually being interrupted by messages about cars or deodorants, and if he or she is given twenty-four hours to think over what he or she has been seeing, the spell can be broken.

King has not been content to let others adapt his work for films. He teamed up with director George Romero to produce *Creepshow* (1982). We will discuss Romero more fully in a moment. *Creepshow* was an instant cult film. It has become one of the best-selling video cassettes. It is funny, gory, and genuinely creepy. It is probably the only film in history that features 40,000 cockroaches.

Creepshow is a collection of five Stephen King stories. They are written and filmed in the style of horror comics that were popular back in the 1950s. The dominant feel of the film is not so much horror as it is horrible humor. King not only wrote the screenplay, he actually starred in one of the episodes. He plays a dumb, greedy farmer. That may be a first for a writer of horror stories.

Writers of screenplays rarely become famous. Have you ever heard of Curt Siodmak? Unless you are a real film buff, you probably haven't. Yet he wrote many of the best horror films of the 1940s, like *I Walked With a Zombie* and *The Wolf Man.*

How about Guy Endore? He was one of the most productive writers of horror film scripts in the 1930s. He wrote *Mad Love* and *Mark of the Vampire.* He also wrote a fine horror novel, *The Werewolf of Paris.* It is one of the best werewolf novels ever written. Hammer turned it into *Curse of the Werewolf,* perhaps the best werewolf film ever made.

One script writer who became more famous than anything he wrote was Rod Serling. Serling was a television, rather than a film, script writer. His series *The Twilight Zone* has some of the best horror episodes ever shown on TV. Even though the series went off the air in 1964, it has remained popular. Reruns can still be seen in many areas, even today. It was also the basis for a major film in 1983.

Serling was not strictly a writer of horror. Many of his *Twilight Zone* scripts were fantasy or science fiction. But all his best shows had a weird or macabre twist.

Serling didn't write all the *Twilight Zone* scripts himself. He did write many of the best ones. He also introduced each episode of the series. He had an impressive screen personality and a fine voice. Rod Serling imitators still turn up in ads, and the phrase "twilight zone" has become part of our vocabulary.

In 1970, a few years after *Twilight Zone* went off the

air, Serling returned with a new series. It was called *Night Gallery*. This series leaned even more heavily toward supernatural horror. It was never quite as successful as *Twilight Zone*. Serling had a lot of trouble with sponsors and censors, who kept changing the scripts. Still, it had some dandy and chilling episodes. It's a shame that series is not rerun more often.

Rod Serling died in 1975. He was only fifty years old. In his career, he had given TV audiences some of the best original horror drama they have ever seen. There is no writer working in television today who can match him.

There have been a number of directors who are best known for directing horror films. Some of these directors have been very important to the development of horror films.

Tod Browning's films span both the silent and sound era. He was one of Lon Chaney's favorite directors in the silent era. When sound came in, he directed the first famous sound horror film. That was, of course, *Dracula.*

Probably the best director of the golden era of horror movies — the 1930s — was *Frankenstein* director James Whale. Whale did only four major horror films: *Frankenstein, The Old Dark House, The Invisible Man* and *Bride of Frankenstein*. Each was splendid. Whale was a director of great intelligence, taste, and humor. While filming *Bride,* Whale had a lot of trouble with the studio. Some of the executives thought that he made the monster too human. Even Karloff thought so. Time has proved that Whale was right. But after *Bride,* he abandoned horror films.

James Whale was a strange, very private man. He directed a number of other very successful nonhorror films. Then, in 1941 he suddenly retired. Later he tried a comeback as director, but this failed. In 1957, James Whale was found floating in his swimming pool — dead.

The 1940s was the era of Val Lewton. Lewton was not a director, but a producer. But all of the nine films that he made bear his very individual stamp. Lewton was hired by RKO to make a series of low-budget horror films. He told his staff, "They may think I'm going to do the usual chiller stuff which will make a quick profit, be laughed at, and be forgotten, but I'm going to make the kind of suspense movie I like."

The kind of movies Lewton liked were those that relied on imagination. He thought that people could be more frightened by what they imagined than by anything that could be shown on the screen. Very rarely are horrible things actually shown in a Lewton film. The viewer is left to imagine what is happening out there in the dark, or just off screen.

Lewton's formula sounds like a recipe for financial disaster in Hollywood. It wasn't. His films were all successful. Not huge successes like *Frankenstein*, but then they didn't cost nearly as much to make either. All his nine films were solid money-makers. And they were a hit with the critics as well. Even today, some Lewton films such as *Cat People* and *I Walked With a Zombie* still attract a large and loyal following.

Lewton died suddenly in 1951. It is impossible to predict where the horror film would have gone if he had lived. As it turned out, the early fifties were dominated by science fiction films which featured such things as giant ants. There were also the gimmick films, 3-D and the rest. And there were the teenage exploitation films like *I Was a Teenage Frankenstein* (1957) and *I Was a Teenage Werewolf* (1957).

By the late 1950s, Hammer Studios in England had begun its cycle of horror remakes. The man who directed most of these was Terence Fisher.

During the 1950s and early 1960s, the American director and producer Roger Corman was getting a reputation for turning out pictures more quickly and cheaply than anyone else. Most of his films appealed to teenagers. They were rock and roll musicals, or hot-rod films. He also did an occasional quickie horror film like *Bucket of Blood* (1959). Then in 1960 he began using Edgar Allan Poe. He began turning Poe stories into films, usually with Vincent Price as his star.

For a director who had been filming rock concerts and freeways as background, directing a Poe story was quite a change. His characters dressed in old-fashioned costumes rather than leather jackets. They wandered around cobwebby old castles and mansions. And compared to the nonstop action of his earlier films, Corman's Poe films were slow. But they were a hit at the box office. They attracted the same sort of teenage audience that had gone to the rock-and-roll films. And the critics, who had hated Corman's other films, responded more kindly to the Poe series.

As I have said, the Hammer horrors were much more

violent than the horror films that had been made before. During the 1970s, there was another and greater explosion of violence in horror films. Many of the films made today make the old Hammer films look tame. The credit, or blame, for this change belongs mainly to three young directors.

In 1968, a young filmmaker from Pittsburgh scraped together some $70,000 to make a little horror film. He had a hard time finding theaters that would show the film. It wound up on the bottom of double bills at drive-ins, or at cheap movie houses that showed triple features. Horror film fans stumbled on it by accident. They were either shocked or delighted or both. Usually both. As word of the film spread, people began lining up to see it. Today the film has made millions. It's still being played at midnight shows. Video cassettes of the film are extremely popular for home viewing. The Museum of Modern Art in New York has made the film part of its permanent film collection.

The name of the film is *Night of the Living Dead*. The director, writer, cinematographer, film editor and just about everything else is George Romero. The film is about zombielike creatures that return from the dead in order to make meals out of the living. No gentle bloodsucking here. These creatures gobble up their victims whole.

The film is graphic and gruesome. Romero shows those eating scenes close up. One of those who put money into the film was a butcher. He also supplied some of the props. *Night of the Living Dead* has some touches of humor. When it first was discovered, movie-goers considered it a real shocker. Today many more gruesome things have been shown in films. *Night of the Living Dead* no longer has the same impact, and it seems a lot funnier than it once did.

In spite of the enormous success of *Night of the Living Dead*, Romero has never "gone Hollywood." He has stayed in Pittsburgh. And he continues to produce his pictures independently. One of his films is *Dawn of the Dead*, the sequel to *Night*. A third film about the zombies is planned for some time in the future. His biggest and most expensive venture to date is *Creepshow*. "I would call it a comedy," says Romero. "But that would be bad for business." Romero thinks people want to scream more than they want to laugh.

Night does not seem as shocking at it once did. But *The Texas Chain Saw Massacre* (1974) is still every bit as shocking. The title gives you a pretty good idea of what the picture is about. Everyone who has ever seen it agrees that it is a thoroughly revolting film. Preview audiences who didn't know anything about the film practically rioted when it was shown to them. The film is relentlessly and realistically sadistic and violent. There is no humor in it.

Yet the film turned out to be one of the top money-makers of 1974. And it has continued to regularly attract audiences. There have, of course, been plenty of other gory films. The difference is that unlike most of the quickie shockers, *Chain Saw* is well made. You may hate the content. I do. But it gets the job done, even if the job is to sicken you.

The man responsible for this film is director Tobe Hooper. Hooper didn't begin the trend toward increasingly violent horror films. But with the success of *Chain Saw*, he certainly speeded it up. Like him or not, Hooper became a major force in the development of horror movies in the seventies.

It was something of a surprise when Hooper was chosen by Steven Spielberg to direct a film. Spielberg had certainly scared us out of the water with *Jaws*. But *Jaws* was vastly different from *Chain Saw*.

I admit to going to see the Hooper-Spielberg film with some uneasiness. The film was *Poltergeist* (1982). It had some frightening, and even slightly revolting, scenes in it. But overall, *Poltergeist* was a charming, extremely enjoyable supernatural horror story. I was pleasantly surprised and greatly relieved. The film has also been very successful.

Undoubtedly the most influential director of horror films of the late 1970s and early 1980s is John Carpenter. He was the creator of the film *Halloween*. The reasons for his influence can be read in dollars and cents. The film cost about $20,000 to make. To date, it has earned over $50 million. And it has spawned several successful sequels, and a host of imitators.

There is a great deal of violence in this film. Stabbings and stranglings are seen up close. But at its core, *Halloween* is an old-fashioned monster movie. The setting is a small town in Illinois, not some ruined castle in Transylvania. The villain is supposed to be a madman named Michael. Like the monsters of old, Michael is nearly impossible to kill. Stab him, shoot him, and just when you think he's dead, he's after you again. He even comes back for sequels. He pursues the girls. But so did Dracula. *Halloween*'s not realistic. It's a fantasy. That's why it is a lot easier to take than *Chain Saw.*

John Carpenter knows how to make a good horror film. Along with the violence there is also atmosphere, real suspense, and even a bit of humor.

Yes, horror films have changed since Bela Lugosi first stepped out of the darkness to say "Good E-e-e-evening." Now there is not only sound, there is color. There are special effects that pioneer horror film directors would never have dreamed of. And, yes, there is more graphic violence — more blood and gore.

But are audiences today more scared than they were back in the 1930s? I don't think so. Today's audiences expect more realistic-looking films. But they still know that the blood isn't real. A horror film can't depend only on mass murder and special effects. It still needs a good script, good directing, and good acting. That's the way it has always been. That's the way it will always be.

iNDEX

Numbers in *italics* indicate photos
of the person or movie listed.

116